new kitchen design

daab

Los fuegos que antaño se encendían en las cocinas tradicionales designaban el hogar desde la Antigüedad; posteriormente, este espacio íntimo en el cual se habitaba y en donde el ser humano desarrollaba sus tareas domésticas y disfrutaba del calor de la lumbre fue llamado vivienda, lugar también para reunirse e iniciar conversaciones. Por ello se puede considerar la cocina como el corazón del ámbito doméstico. Los tipos de cocina han ido evolucionando con el tiempo y se han ido adaptando a las necesidades de cada época. Los diseños de cocinas actuales de un gran número de países toman como referente el modelo de cocina estadounidense, que se integra en el resto de la casa y ocupa espacios abiertos, tanto en apartamentos con divisiones tradicionales del espacio como en lofts o estudios.

Depuis l'antiquité, les feux qu'on allumait dans les cuisines traditionnelles symbolisaient le foyer; plus tard, cet espace intime dans lequel on vivait et où l'être humain accomplissait ses tâches ménagères et profitait de la chaleur de la flamme fut appelé logis, lieu de réunion où commençaient les conversations. La cuisine peut pour cela être considérée comme étant au coeur du cadre domestique. Au cours de l'histoire, les types de cuisine ont évolué et se sont adaptés aux besoins de chaque époque. Aujourd'hui, dans un grand nombre de pays, le design des cuisines prend la cuisine américaine comme modèle. Celle-ci s'intègre au reste de la maison et occupe des espaces ouverts, que ce soit dans des appartements ayant des séparations traditionnelles ou dans des lofts ou des studios.

I fuochi che una volta venivano accesi nelle cucine tradizionali rappresentavano fin dall'antichità il "focolare"; in seguito, questo spazio intimo nel quale si abitava e dove l'essere umano svolgeva le sue attività domestiche e godeva il calore del focolare fu chiamato abitazione, luogo per riunirsi ed iniziare una conversazione. Per questo si può considerare la cucina come il cuore dell'ambito domestico. I tipi di cucina si sono evoluti nel tempo e si sono adattati alle necessità di ogni epoca. La progettazione delle cucine attuali di un gran numero di paesi prende come riferimento il modello della cucina statunitense, che si integra nel resto della casa ed occupa spazi aperti, sia in appartamenti con divisioni tradizionali dello spazio che in lofts o monolocali.

Seit der Antike ist für die Menschen das Herdfeuer der primitiven Kochstellen gleichbedeutend mit Heimstatt. Später bildete sich um den Herd und die Küche herum der Wohnraum der Menschen, der Platz, an dem sie Wärme suchten, ihre häuslichen Verrichtungen erledigten, sich im Schein des Feuers Geschichten erzählten und Erfahrungen austauschten. Die Küche gilt daher als das Herzstück der Wohnung. Die Küchenausstattung hat sich im Laufe der Zeit den sich wandelnden Bedürfnissen und Anforderungen jeder Epoche angepasst. Heutzutage folgt man vielfach dem nordamerikanischen Modell einer offenen Küche, die sich in die Wohnung integriert, und zwar sowohl in Wohnungen traditionellen Ausmaßes als auch in großflächigen Wohnräumen wie Studios oder Lofts.

The fires lit long ago inside traditional kitchens defined the concept of home since antiquity. Thereafter, this intimate space in which man abided and carried out household chores in the comforting warmth of the fire came to be called the home, serving as a gathering place and a setting for conversation. For this reason, the kitchen can be considered the heart of any domestic space. Kitchen types have evolved over time and adapted to the needs of each time period. Today, kitchen designs from a great number of countries look to the model of the American kitchen, characterized by its open-plan scheme and its integration into traditional apartments, lofts or studios.

Arteks | Andorra la Vella, Principat d´Andorra
Kitchen for a Family
Andorra la Vella, Principat d´Andorra | 2003

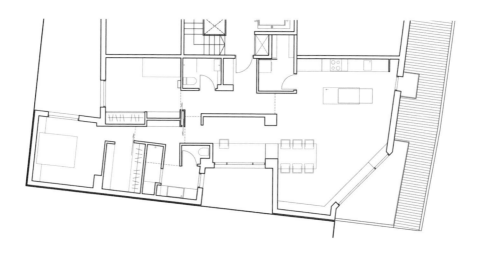

Arthur Collins | London, UK
C Apartment
London, UK | 2003

Ash Sakula Architects | London, UK
House in Mecklenburg Square
London, UK | 2002

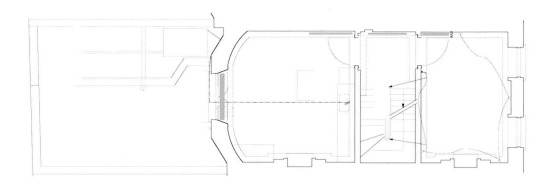

Ayhan Ozan, AIA | New York, USA
Silver & Brown
New York, USA | 2003

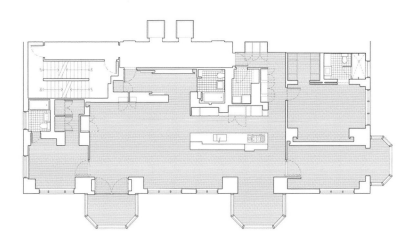

Baratloo-Balch Architects | New York, USA
Friedrich-Vollhardt Loft
New York, USA | 2003

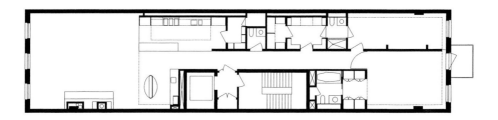

Bembé + Dellinger Architects | Greifenberg, Germany
B & D Apartment
Greifenberg, Germany | 2002

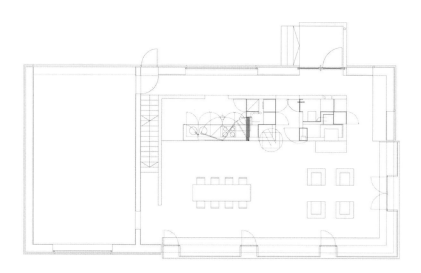

Carlo Donati | Milan, Italy
Loft A
Milan, Italy | 2001

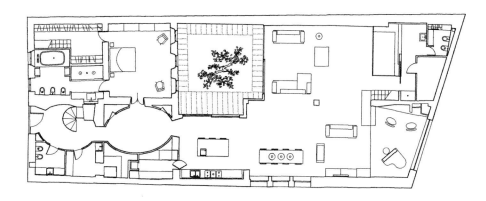

Carlos Mir | Barcelona, Spain
Apartment in Barcelona
Barcelona, Spain | 2002

Chavanne & Holzer Design | Vienna, Austria

Villa in Vienna
Vienna, Austria | 2003

Child Graddon Lewis | London, UK
Loft in London
London, UK | 2000

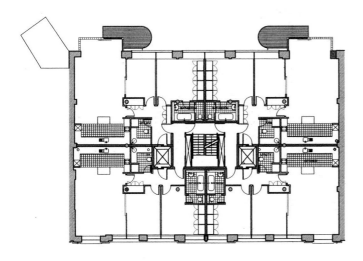

CZWG Architects | London, UK
Fulham Island
Fulham Island, UK | 2003

Detail Architects | London, UK
Loft in Surrey
Surrey, UK | 2000

Estudio Olatz de Ituarte | Barcelona, Spain
The Island
Barcelona, Spain | 2003

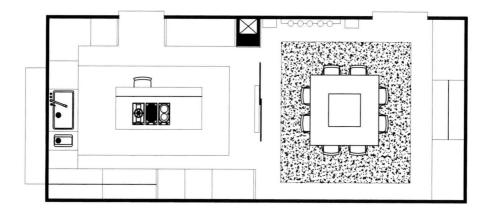

Fátima Vilaseca | Barcelona, Spain
Glass
Barcelona, Spain | 2003

Feyferlik-Fritzer | Graz, Austria
R House
Graz, Austria | 2003

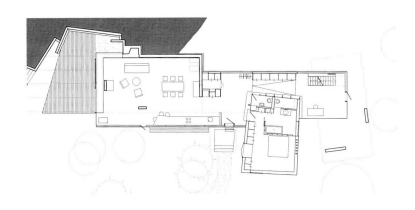

Florence Lim | London, UK
Florence Lim House
London, UK | 2003

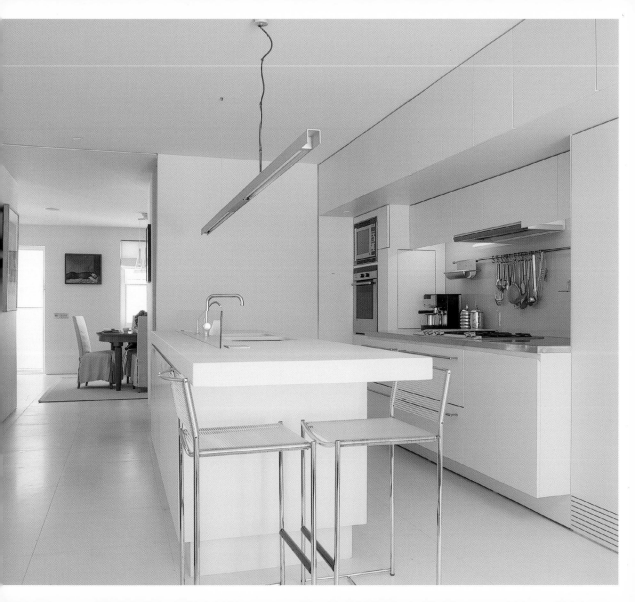

Gianvittorio Plazzogna for Elmar Cucine | Biancade, Italy
Antracite
Biancade, Italy | 2004

Guard Tillman Pollock / Mark Guard | London, UK
Bankside Lofts
London, UK | 2003

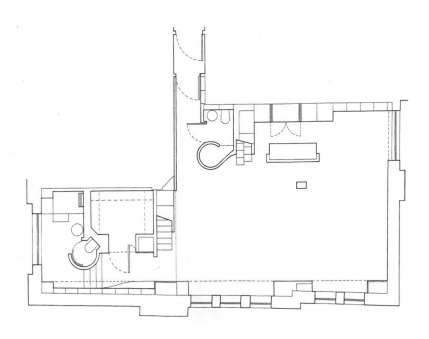

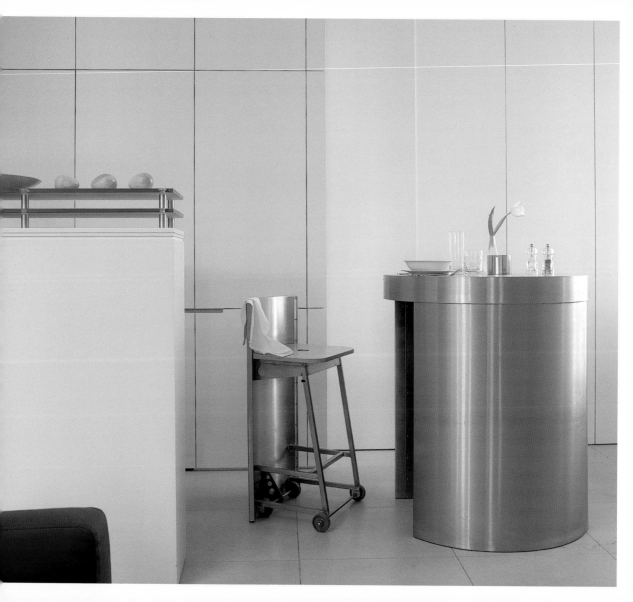

Héctor Restrepo Calvo. Heres Arquitectura | Barcelona, Spain
Red Sensations
Barcelona, Spain | 2003

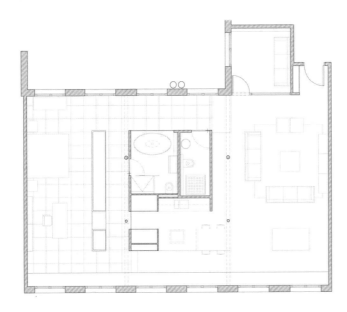

High Touch | Tel Aviv, Israel
Blue Kitchen
Tel Aviv, Israel | 2004

Ivans Bussens | London, UK
Apartment in London
London, UK | 2003

Jeffrey McKean Architect | New York, USA
Manhattan Apartment
New York, USA | 2002

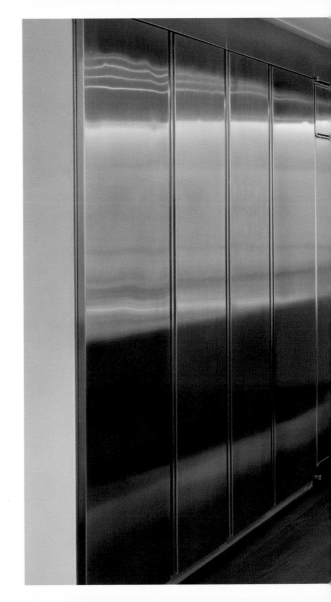

Joan Bach | Barcelona, Spain
Vallromanes House
Barcelona, Spain | 2002

Josep M.ª Font for Greek | Barcelona, Spain
Flat in Aribau Street
Barcelona, Spain | 2003

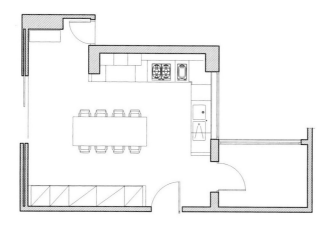

Lewis.Tsurumaki.Lewis | New York, USA
Loft Geltner Parker
New York, USA | 2001

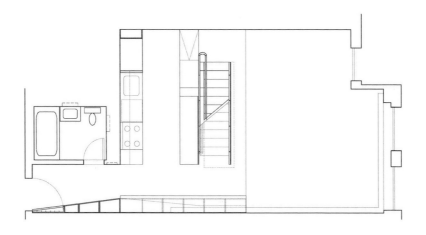

Lucy Humbly, Interior Designer | London, England

The Bridge Penthouse
London, UK | 2003

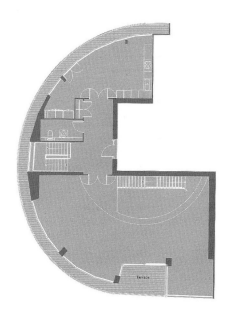

Manuel Serrano Arquitectos | Madrid, Spain
Quevedo Loft
Madrid, Spain | 2004

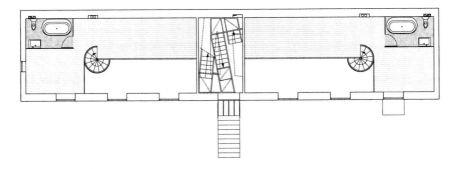

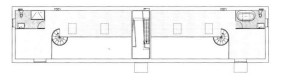

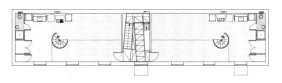

Messana O´Rorke Architects | New York, USA
Blaire O´Brien Kitchen
New York, USA | 2003

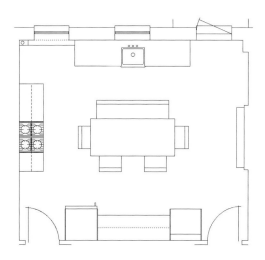

Mike Tonkins | London, UK
White & Red
London, UK | 2003

Nardi Architecture | Paris, France
House in Firenze
Firenze, Italy | 2003

Oskar Leo Kaufmann | Vorarlberg, Austria
Susi K
Vorarlberg, Austria | 2003

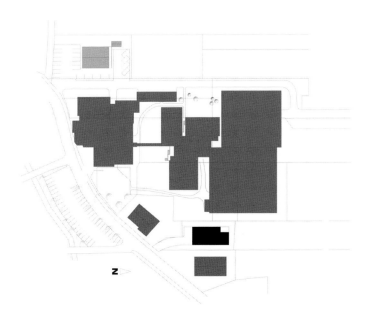

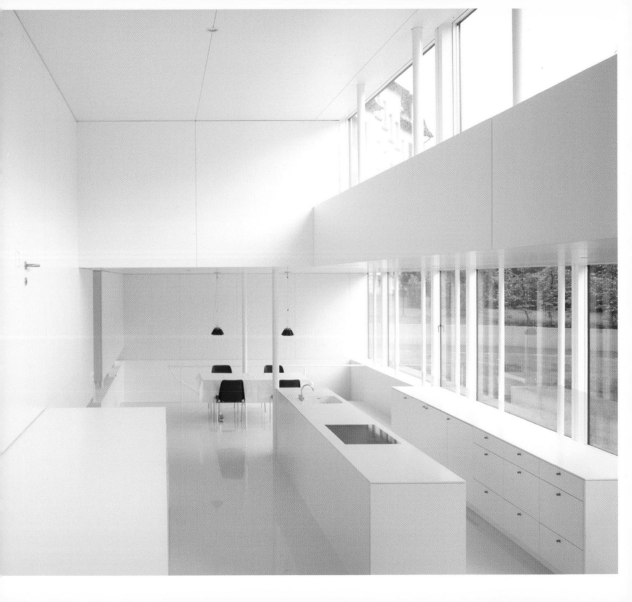

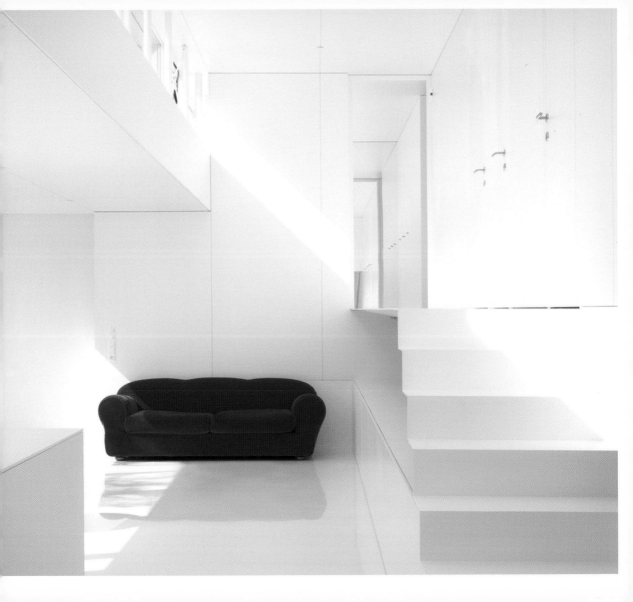

Pablo Fernández Lorenzo and Pablo Redondo Díez | Madrid, Spain
Flat in Madrid
Madrid, Spain | 2003

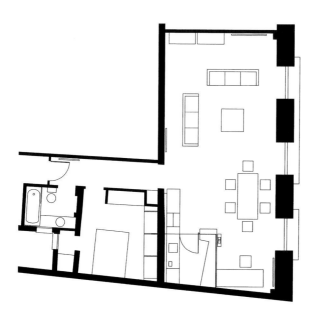
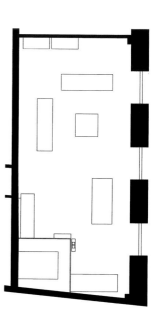

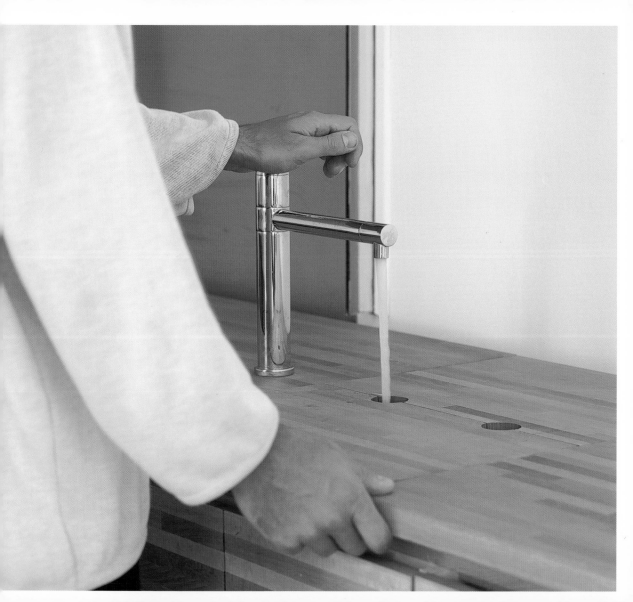

Pedini SRL | London, UK
Open Kitchen
London, UK | 2002

Philippe Starck's Studio | Paris, France
Flat in Buenos Aires
Buenos Aires, Argentina | 2003

Ramón Pintó, Arquitecto | Barcelona, Spain
House in Cabrera de Mar
Barcelona, Spain | 2003

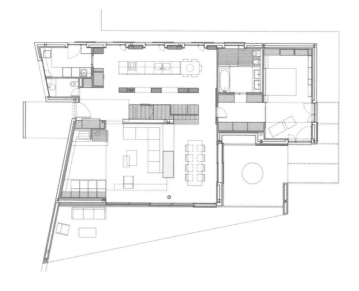

Roger Bellera | Girona, Spain
Poblenou Loft
Barcelona, Spain | 2003

Ronnette Riley Architect | New York, USA
East Side Residence
New York, USA | 2001

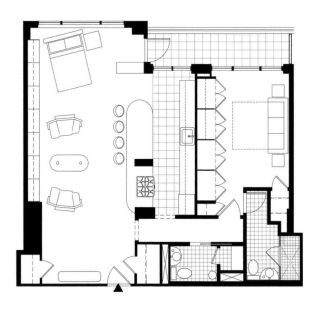

Ruhl Walker | Boston, USA
Hunter-Ritacco Loft
Boston, USA | 2002

Sara Colledge | London, UK
Flat in London
London, UK | 2003

Takao Shiotsuka Atelier | Oita, Japan
N Guesthouse
Oita, Japan | 2003

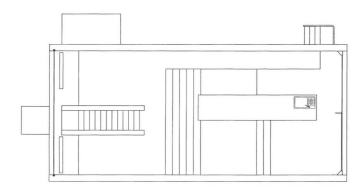

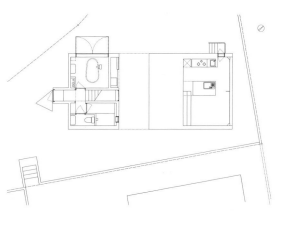

Werner Sobek | Stuttgart, Germany
House in Stuttgart
Stuttgart, Germany | 2002

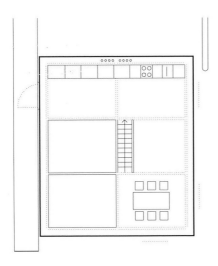

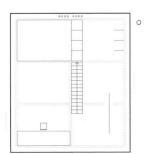

Arteks
C/ L'aigüeta 12, 1°, Andorra la Vella, Principat d´Andorra
P +37 682 32 02
F +37 682 32 72
arteks@andorra.ad
Kitchen for a Family
Photos: © Eugeni Pons

Arthur Collins / Studios Architecture
33 Gresse Street, London, W1V 9LD, UK
P +44 020 7323 0332
C Apartment
Photos: © View / Richard Glover

Ash Sakula Architects
24 Rosebery Avenue, London EC1R 4SX, UK
P +44 020 7837 9735
F +44 020 7837 9708
www.ashak.com
info@ashak.com
House in Mecklenburg Square
Photos: © View / Edmund Sumner

Ayhan Ozan, AIA
Chelsea Atelier Architect, PC
245 7th Avenue, suite 6A, New York, NY 10001, USA
P +01 212 255 3494
F +01 212 255 3495
Silver & Brown
Photos: © Björg

Baratloo-Balch Architects
155 West 88th Street, New York, NY 10024, USA
P +1 212 873 64 50
Friedrich-Vollhardt Loft
Photos: © Jordi Miralles

Bembé + Dellinger
Am Schloß, 86926 Greifenberg, Germany
P +81 92 99 99 12
www.bembe-dellinger.de
mail@bembe-dellinger.de
B & D Apartment
Photos: © Artur / Stefan Mueller-Naumann

Carlo Donati
Via Appiani 5, 20121 Milan, Italy
P +39 02 29006138
carlodon@tiscalinet.it
Loft A
Photos: © Matteo Piazza

Carlos Mir
C/ Marqués de Monistrol 17, 08960 Sant Just Desvern
Barcelona, Spain
P +34 934 733 124
F +34 934 700 629
Carlosmir@retemail.es
Apartment in Barcelona
Photos: © Montse Garriga

Chavanne & Holzer Design
Schönbrunnerstr 31, A-1050 Vienna, Austria
P +43 (1) 97 413 21
F +43 (1) 97 413 61
chavanne@chello.at
florian.holzer@aon.at
Villa in Vienna
Photos : © René Chavanne

Child Graddon Lewis
Studio 1, 155 Commercial Street, London E1 63J, UK
P +44 (0)20 75391200
F +44 (0)20 75391201
www.cgluk.com
Loft in London
Photos: © View / Dennis Gilbert

CZWG Architects
17 Bowling Green Lane, London, EC1R OBD, UK
P +44 020 7253 2523
mail@czwgarchitects.co.uk
Fulham Island
Photos: © View / Grant Smith

Detail Architects
D2 Metropolitan Wharf, Wapping Wall, London E1W 3SS, UK
P +44 020 7488 1669
www.detail.co.uk
Loft in Surrey
Photos: © Jonathan Moore

Estudio Olatz de Ituarte
C/ Freixa 42, Bajos, 08021 Barcelona, Spain
P +34 93 200 90 16
F +34 93 414 27 71
olatzitu@teleline.es
The Island
Photos: © Montse Garriga

Fátima Vilaseca
Barcelona, Spain
P +34 629 72 53 35
Glass
Photos: © Montse Garriga

Feyferlik-Fritzer
Glacisstraße 7, 8010 Graz, Austria
P +43 316 34 76 56
F +43 316 38 29 60
feyferlik@inode.at
fritzer@inode.cc
R House
Photos: © Paul Ott

Florence Lim
London, UK
Florence Lim House
Photos: © Red Cover / Henry Wilson

Gianvittorio Plazzogna for Elmar Cucine
Via E. Salgari 18, 31030 Biancade (Treviso), Italy
P +04 22 84 91 42
F +04 22 84 97 89
www.elmarcucine.com
elmar@elmarcucine.com
Antracite
Photos: © Elmar Cucine

Guard Tillman Pollock / Mark Guard
161 Whitfield Street, London W1T 5ET, UK
P +44 (0) 20 73 80 11 99
F +44 (0) 20 73 87 54 41
www.markguard.com
info@markguard.com
Bankside Lofts
Photos: © Red Cover / Henry Wilson

Héctor Restrepo Calvo. Heres Arquitectura
C/ Bisbe Sivilla 38-40, Sobreático, 08022 Barcelona, Spain
P/F +34 93 417 28 95
heres@arquired.es
Red Sensations
Photos: © Nuria Fuentes

High Touch
Tel Aviv, Israel
Blue Kitchen
Photos: © Yael Pincus

Ivans Bussens
2.3 York Central, 70 York Way, London, N1 9AG, UK
P +44 020 79 33 50 66
Apartment in London
Photos: © View / Richard Glover

Jeffrey McKean Architect
135 West Broadway, New York, NY 10013, USA
P +1 212 964 23 00
F +1 212 964 23 10
www.jeffreymckean.com
Manhattan Apartment
Photos: © Björg

Joan Bach
Barcelona, Spain
P +34 93 488 19 25
Vallromanes House
Photos: © Jordi Miralles

Josep Mª Font for Greek
C/ Rubinstein 4, 08022 Barcelona, Spain
P +34 93 418 95 50
F +34 93 418 95 32
www.greekbcn.com
Flat in Aribau Street
Photos: © Montse Garriga

Lewis.Tsurumaki.Lewis
147 Essex Street, New York, NY 10002, USA
P +1 212 505 5955
www.ltlwork.net
Loft Geltner Parker
Photos: © Lewis.Tsurumaki.Lewis

Lucy Humbly, Interior Designer
Aria House, 23 Craven Street (London Town),
London WC2N 5NT, UK
P +44 207 839 5588
www.londontownplc.co.uk
info@londontowngroup.co.uk
The Bridge Penthouse
Photos: © Carlos Domínguez

Manuel Serrano Arquitectos
C/ Padilla 54 bis, 28006 Madrid, Spain
P +34 91 309 36 35
F +34 91 309 39 33
serrano-arquitectos@usa.net
Quevedo Loft
Photos: © José Latova

Messana O´Rorke Architects
118 West 22nd St, 9 floor, New York, NY 10011, USA
P +1 212 807 19 60
F +1 212 807 19 66
www.messanaororke.com
Blaire O´Brian Kitchen
Photos: © Elizabeth Felicella

Mike Tonkins
London, UK
White & Red
Photos: © Red Cover / Winfried Heinze

Nardi Architecture
Paris, France
House in Firenze
Photos: © Guy Bouchet / Ana Cardinale

Oskar Leo Kaufmann
Steinebach 3, 6850 Dornbirn, Vorarlberg, Austria
P +43 (0) 55 72 39 49 69
www.olk.cc
office@olk.cc
Susi K
Photos: © Adolf Bereuter

Pablo Fernández Lorenzo and Pablo Redondo Díez
C/ San Marcos 3, 3° 3ª, 28004 Madrid, Spain
P +34 91 521 95 82
pablofl@coam.es
Flat in Madrid
Photos: © Eugeni Pons

Pedini SRL
Via Aspio 8, 61030 Lucrezia di Catoceto (PU), Italy
P +39 0721 899988
F +39 0721 899955
www.pedini.it
info@pedini.it
Open Kitchen
Photos: © Red Cover / Jake Fitzjones

Philippe Starck´s Studio
18-20, rue du Faubourg du Temple, 75001 Paris, France
P +33 (0) 1 48 07 54 54
F +33 (0) 1 48 07 54 64
www.philippe-starck.com
info@philippe-starck.com
Flat in Buenos Aires
Photos: © Ricardo Labougle / Ana Cardinale

Ramón Pintó, Arquitecto
Avenida Pau Casals 7, Sat. 2ª, 08021 Barcelona, Spain
P +34 93 414 10 61
ramonpinto@coac.es
House in Cabrera de Mar
Photos: © Jordi Miralles

Roger Bellera
Plaça de l'Església s/n., Galeries Begur, Local 3,
17255 Begur, Girona, Spain
P +34 629 78 31 12
Poblenou Loft
Photos: © Jordi Miralles

Ronnette Riley Architect
350 Fith Avenue, suite 8001, New York, NY 10118, USA
P +1 212 594 4015
F +1 212 594 2668
www.ronnetteriley.com
East Side Residence
Photos: © Dub Rogers

Ruhl Walker
60K Street, Boston, MA 02127, USA
P +1 617 268 54 79
F +1 617 268 54 82
www.ruhlwalker.com
Hunter-Ritacco Loft
Photo: © Jordi Miralles

Sara Colledge
London, UK
Flat in London
Photos: © Red Cover / Guglielmo Galvin

Takao Shiotsuka Atelier
5-1 Mitsuyoshi-shinmati, Oita-shi, 870.1135 Oita, Japan
P +81 97 503 95 05
F +81 97 503 95 06
www.shio-atl.com
shio-atl@shio-atl.com
N Guesthouse
Photos: © Kaori Ichikawa

Werner Sobek Ingenieure GmbH & Co.
KG, Albstr. 14, 70597 Stuttgart, Germany
P +49 (0)711 76750 38
F +49 (0)711 76750 44
www.wernersobek.com
frank.heinlein@wernersobek.com
House in Stuttgart
Photos: © Artur / Roland Halbe

© 2006 daab
cologne london new york

published and distributed worldwide by
daab gmbh
friesenstr. 50
d-50670 köln

p +49-221-94 10 740
f +49-221-94 10 741

mail@daab-online.com
www.daab-online.com

publisher ralf daab
rdaab@daab-online.com

creative director feyyaz
mail@feyyaz.com

editorial project by loft publications
© 2006 loft publications

editor encarna castillo
layout diego gonzález
english translation ana cristina g. cañizares
french translation jean pierre layre cassou
italian translation grazia suffritti
german translation martin fischer
copy editing raquel vicente durán

printed in spain
gráfiques iberia, spain

isbn 3-937718-15-X
d.l. B-18672-06